SUPERCARS

# LAMBORGHINI

Ryan Smith

www.av2books.com

AV2

**Step 1**
Go to **www.av2books.com**

**Step 2**
Enter this unique code
**GMPYU0GD3**

**Step 3**
Explore your interactive eBook!

**AV2 is optimized for use on any device**

# Your interactive eBook comes with...

**Contents**
Browse a live contents page to easily navigate through resources

**Audio**
Listen to sections of the book read aloud

**Videos**
Watch informative video clips

**Weblinks**
Gain additional information for research

**Try This!**
Complete activities and hands-on experiments

**Key Words**
Study vocabulary, and complete a matching word activity

**Quizzes**
Test your knowledge

**Slideshows**
View images and captions

## ... and much, much more!

SUPERCARS

# LAMBORGHINI

# CONTENTS

# LAMBO

RGHINI

# LAMBORGHINI SUPERCARS

Supercars are more than just **luxurious** sports cars. A supercar is the combination of the latest technology and designs that make a statement. All of the effort and care that goes into building a supercar means that only so many are built each year. This means that supercars are **exclusive**. Because supercars are exclusive, they can cost hundreds of thousands of dollars. Over time, exclusive cars can become collectors' items.

The **Lamborghini Veneno** was so **exclusive** that it had a starting price of **$4.5 million**.

Since 1963, Lamborghini has been finding new ways to make supercars faster and more powerful. The iconic shape and sound of a Lamborghini cannot be missed as it speeds down the road.

The Lamborghini factory produces **8,000 cars a year**.

# FERRUCCIO LAMBORGHINI

***"I never planned on getting into the automobile industry, but I knew a better car could be built."***
–Ferruccio Lamborghini

Ferruccio Lamborghini was a fan of supercars. One of his cars was a white Ferrari. Ferruccio had ideas about how to make Ferrari's cars better. When Enzo Ferrari said that he did not want to work with Ferruccio, Ferruccio decided to build supercars on his own.

Ferruccio was already a successful businessman when he started his car company. He had made most of his money from a company that built tractors. Ferruccio wanted to use his success to build the perfect supercar. After just a few months, Ferruccio was unveiling incredible cars at international **auto shows**.

Ferruccio's tractor company, Lamborghini Trattori, still makes tractors today.

# MAP OF ITALY

**Ferruccio Lamborghini fixed tractors on his family's farm outside of Cento, Italy.**

# THE RAGING BULL

Ferruccio was born on April 28, 1916. This meant his **zodiac sign** was Taurus, the bull. Ferruccio chose to use a raging bull on his logo as a way to represent himself. He also thought a raging bull represented the power of his cars. The background of the first Lamborghini logo was red. This was done to get the attention of Lamborghini's rival, Ferrari. The color of the background was later changed to black.

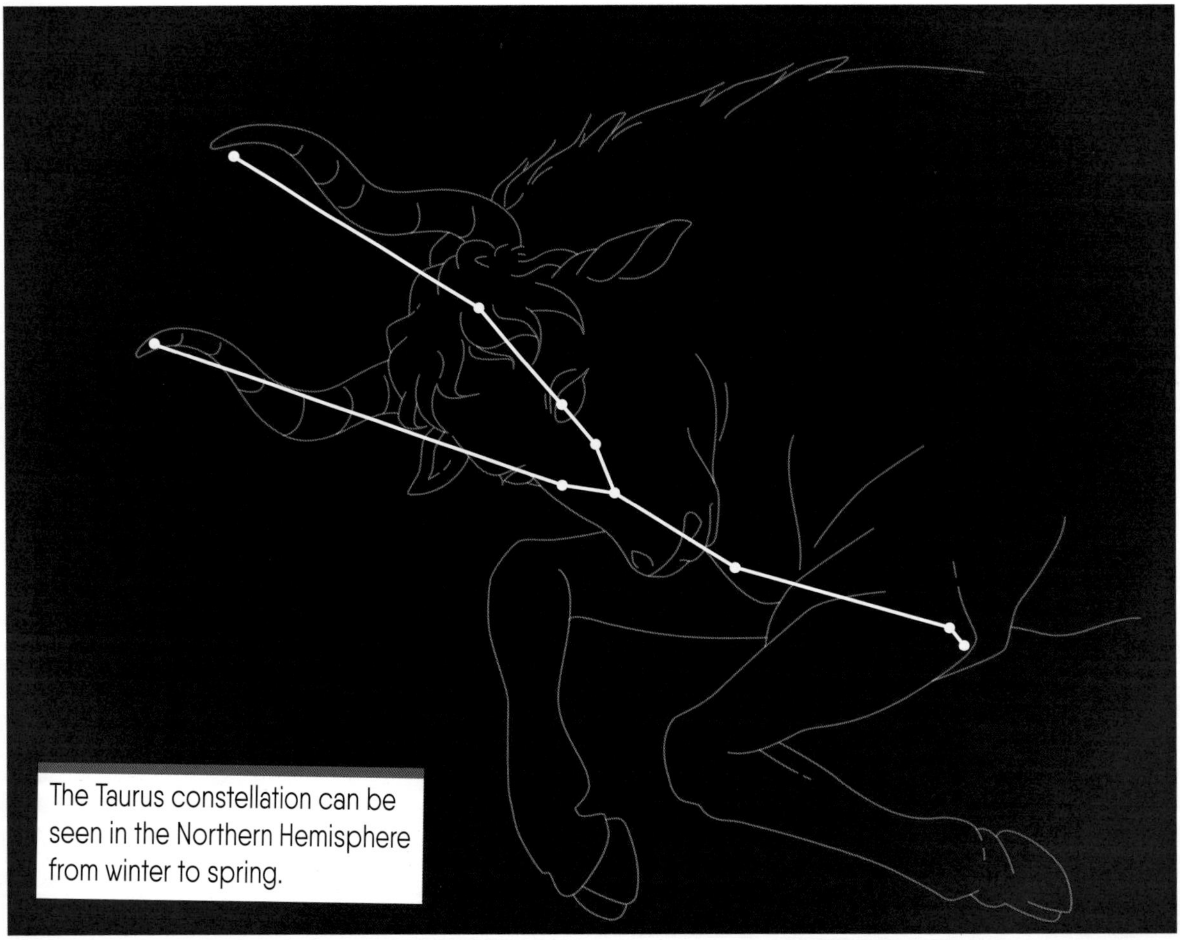

The Taurus constellation can be seen in the Northern Hemisphere from winter to spring.

# LAMBORGHINI LOGO

Ferruccio Lamborghini's last name runs across the top of the logo.

The charging bull represents power, speed, and dominance.

The background is black to represent power and status.

The logo's gold color represents luxury.

# THROUGH HISTORY

**Ferruccio had a dream of creating the perfect supercar. Today, Lamborghinis are known all over the world for their speed and power.**

The Lamborghini Miura is presented at the Geneva Motor Show. It is the first of many Lamborghinis to be named after a breed of fighting bull.

## 1963

## 1966

## 1986

Ferruccio Lamborghini starts his luxury car company, Automobili Ferruccio Lamborghini.

Lamborghini produces its first off-road vehicle, the Lamborghini LM002.

Lamborghini and the Massachusetts Institute of Technology (MIT) file a **patent** on a new **supercapacitor** material.

The Lamborghini Museum opens at the Lamborghini factory.

2001

2017

2019

Lamborghini releases its super sports utility vehicle (SUV), the Lamborghini Urus.

# FAMOUS LAMBORGHINIS

One famous movie appearance for Lamborghini's cars is in the superhero movie, *Doctor Strange*. The character Dr. Stephen Strange drives a Lamborghini Huracán along a winding road.

Six Lamborghini Huracáns were used in the filming of *Doctor Strange*.

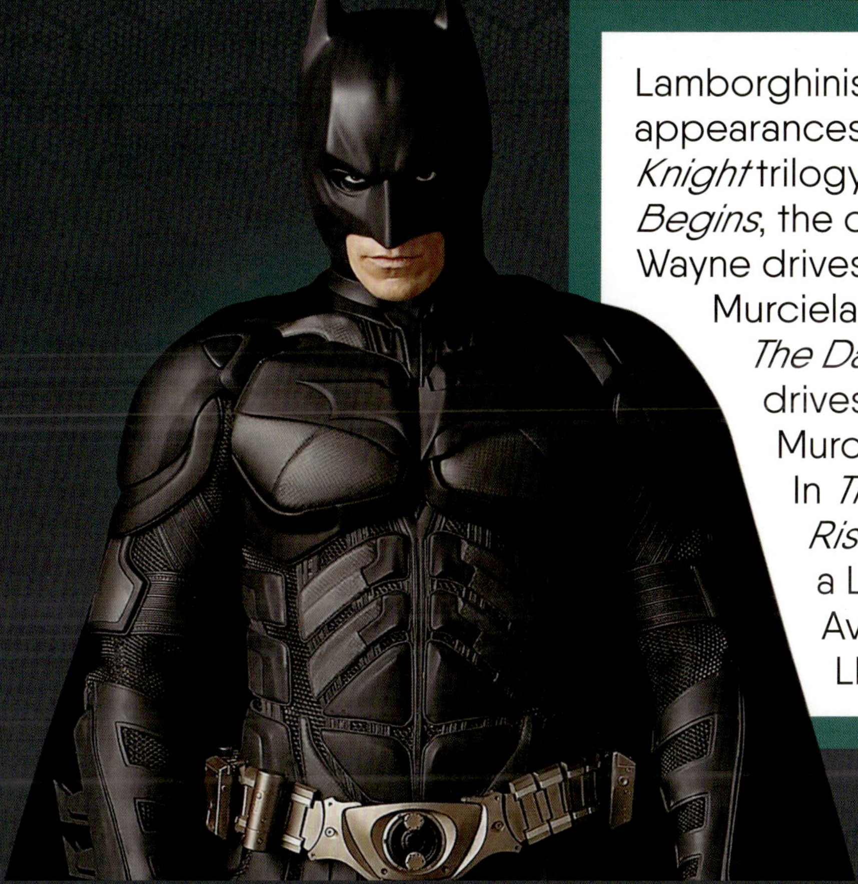

Lamborghinis also make appearances in *The Dark Knight* trilogy. In *Batman Begins*, the character Bruce Wayne drives a Lamborghini Murcielago Roadster. In *The Dark Knight*, Wayne drives a Lamborghini Murcielago LP640. In *The Dark Knight Rises*, he drives a Lamborghini Aventador LP 700-4.

Lamborghini Murcielago Roadster

Lamborghini Murcielago LP640

Lamborghini Aventador LP 700-4

# AT THE RACES

Lamborghini's racing division is called Squadra Corse. *Squadra corse* means "racing team" in Italian. It is made up of different Lamborghini racing programs.

One Squadra Corse racing program supports race teams that use the Huracán GT3 EVO to take part in **Grand Touring (GT)** racing around the world.

Another Squadra Corse racing program is the Lamborghini Super Trofeo race series. The Lamborghini Huracán Super Trofeo Evo is the only **model** of car that takes part in these races.

Prince Albert von Thurn und Taxis, won the 2010 ADAC GT Masters racing series in Germany.

Lamborghini took part in the 2020 Rolex 24 at Daytona endurance race in Daytona Beach, Florida.

The **Huracán set a world record** for a half-mile run, reaching a top speed of **259.67 miles per hour (418 kilometers per hour).**

GEAR Racing is an all-female racing team that drives a Huracán.

The **Huracán GT3** won its **first 24 Hours at Daytona** in **2019**.

Lamborghini won the 2018 Northeast Grand Prix in Lakeville, Connecticut.

# HOW IT'S MADE

The Lamborghini factories are located in Sant'Agata Bolognese, Italy. Every Lamborghini that is built has already been purchased by someone. This allows the factory to customize each Lamborghini for each customer. Customers can visit the factory and watch as their cars are built. In 2015, the factory was certified as being **carbon neutral**.

Lamborghini engines are assembled in the factory.

Technicians work at stations as the cars move down the assembly line.

It takes **300 people** to assemble each **Lamborghini**.

Lamborghini plans to **build 4,000 Lamborghini Uruses** in **2020**.

The cars spend about 30 minutes at each station.

Lamborghinis are closely inspected before they are turned over to each customer.

# TODAY'S LINEUP

Today's Lamborghinis are changing what it means to be a supercar. The Lamborghini Sián FKP 37 is a **hybrid** car that uses an electric motor to create even more power. The Lamborghini Urus is an SUV with all of the power and luxury of a supercar.

Here are some of the Lamborghinis on the road today.

## Lamborghini Urus

Engine: **V8**

Maximum Horsepower: **650**

0–60 mph (0–100 km/h): **3.6 seconds**

Starting Price: **$200,000**

## Lamborghini Huracán EVO Spyder

Engine: **V10**

Maximum Horsepower: **640**

0–60 mph (0–100 km/h): **3.1 seconds**

Starting Price: **$233,000**

## Lamborghini Aventador SVJ

Engine: **V12**

Maximum Horsepower: **770**

0–60 mph (0–100 km/h): **2.8 seconds**

Starting Price: **$518,000**

## Lamborghini Centenario

Engine: **V12**

Maximum Horsepower: **770**

0–60 mph (0–100 km/h): **2.8 seconds**

Starting Price: **$1,900,000**

## Lamborghini Sián FKP 37

Engine: **V12 and 48V electric motor**

Maximum Horsepower: **819**

0–60 mph (0–100 km/h): **2.8 seconds**

Starting Price: **$2,210,000**

# TOMORROW'S LAMBORGHINI

Lamborghini is using its **concept cars** to test designs and technologies that could be used in future cars.

Currently, the Urus is helping Lamborghini reach even more car buyers than ever before. The four door Lamborghini Estoque is a **sedan** concept car that will test if Lamborghini can go even further into the everyday driving market.

Lamborghini is also testing technologies for electric cars. The Lamborghini Asterion is a plug-in hybrid car that has three electric motors. The Lamborghini Terzo Millennio is an electric supercar that is being used to test different ways of storing electricity in the body of a car. It is also being used to test supercapacitors in electric cars.

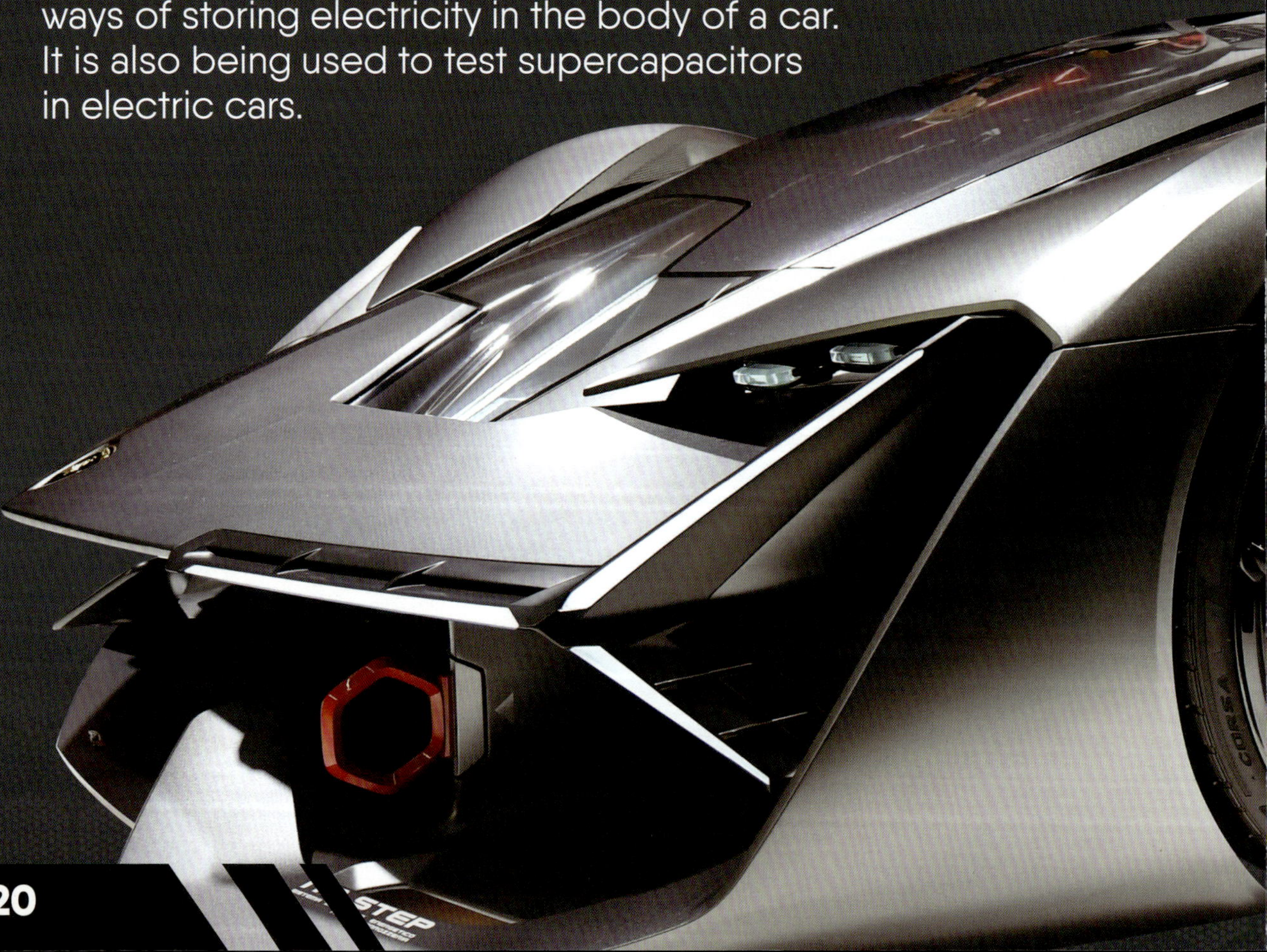

The Terzo Millennio will generate power as it drives.

The Asterion can handle city driving on its electric charge.

A Lamborghini sedan will be produced in 2025.

The Terzo Millennio will have a carbon fiber body in order to make the car lighter and faster.

# LAMBORGHINI QUIZ

1. Lamborghini plans to build 4,000 of which type of Lamborghini in 2020?

2. How did Ferruccio Lamborghini make most of his money before he began to build cars?

3. What is Ferruccio Lamborghini's zodiac sign?

4. In what year did Lamborghini produce its first off-road vehicle?

5. Which Lamborghini appears in *The Dark Knight Rises*?

6. What is Lamborghini's racing division called?

7. Where are the Lamborghini factories?

8. How many people assemble each Lamborghini?

9. Which of today's Lamborghinis uses an electric motor to create more power?

10. Which Lamborghini concept car is being used to test supercapacitors in electric cars?

**ANSWERS**

**1** The Lamborghini Urus **2** A company that built tractors **3** Taurus **4** 1986 **5** A Lamborghini Aventador LP 700-4 **6** Squadra Corse **7** In Sant'Agata Bolognese, Italy **8** 300 **9** Lamborghini Sián FKP 37 **10** The Lamborghini Terzo Millennio

# KEY WORDS

**auto shows:** places where car companies show off their latest designs and concepts

**carbon neutral:** balancing how much carbon dioxide goes into the air with carbon-reducing technologies and programs

**concept cars:** cars built to highlight new technologies and designs

**exclusive:** limited in number

**Grand Touring (GT):** a race car that seats two people

**hybrid:** a car that is powered by both a gas engine and an electric motor

**luxurious:** something that is pleasing and comfortable

**model:** a particular car design made by a company

**patent:** official recognition of ownership for an idea of invention

**sedan:** a car that sits four or more people and has a roof that is fixed in place

**supercapacitor:** a device that can quickly charge and release electricity

**zodiac sign:** a group of stars that are associated with a certain time of year

# INDEX

Published by AV2
14 Penn Plaza, 9th Floor
New York, NY 10122
Website: www.av2books.com



Library of Congress Cataloging-in-Publication Data

Names: Smith, Ryan, author.
Title: Lamborghini / Ryan Smith.
Description: New York, NY : AV2, [2021] | Series: Supercars | Includes index. | Audience: Ages 8-12. | Audience: Grades 4-6.
Identifiers: LCCN 2020016897 (print) | LCCN 2020016898 (ebook) | ISBN 9781791125837 (library binding) | ISBN 9781791125844 (paperback) | ISBN 9781791125851 | ISBN 9781791125868
Subjects: LCSH: Lamborghini automobile--Juvenile literature.
Classification: LCC TL215.L33 S65 2021 (print) | LCC TL215.L33 (ebook) | DDC 629.222--dc23
LC record available at https://lccn.loc.gov/2020016897
LC ebook record available at https://lccn.loc.gov/2020016898

Printed in Guangzhou, China
1 2 3 4 5 6 7 8 9 0 24 23 22 21 20

062020
101119

Art Director: Terry Paulhus Project Coordinator: Ryan Smith

Every reasonable effort has been made to trace ownership and to obtain permission to reprint copyright material. The publisher would be pleased to have any errors or omissions brought to its attention so that they may be corrected in subsequent printings.

The publisher acknowledges Alamy, Getty Images, iStock, Shutterstock, and Wikimedia as its primary image suppliers for this title.